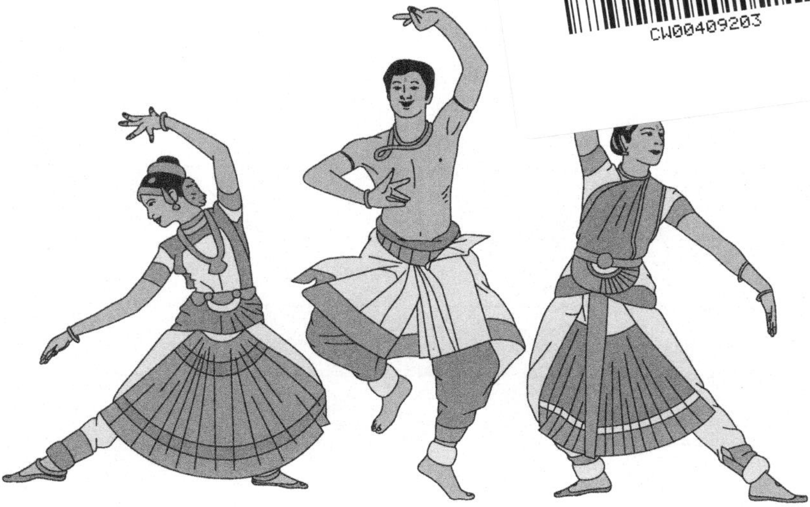

This Book Belongs To

____

____

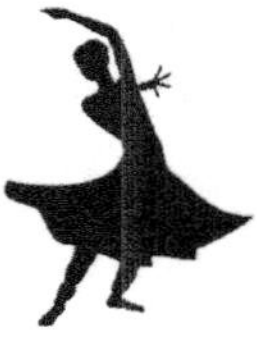

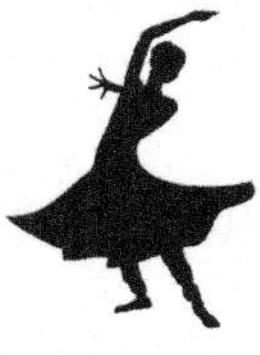

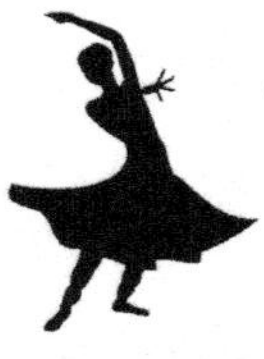

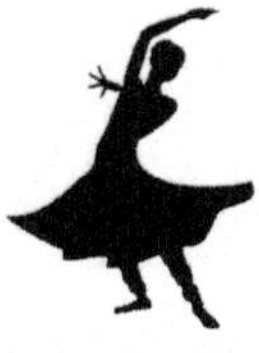

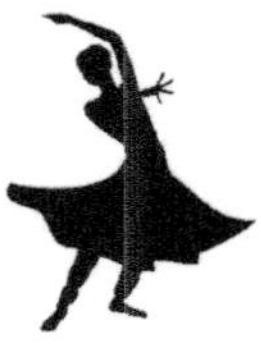

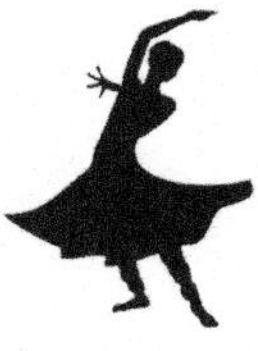

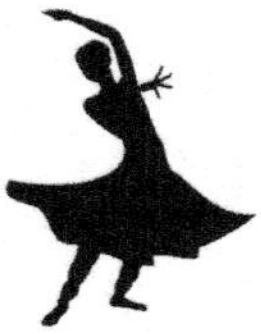

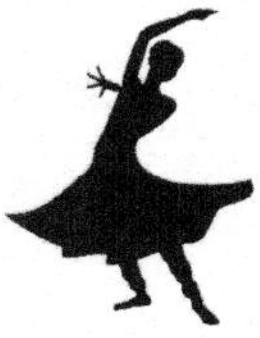

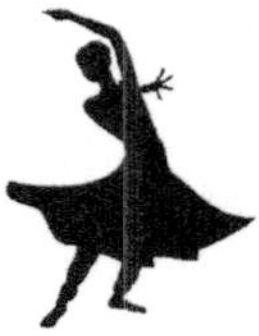

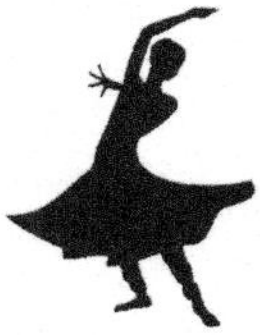

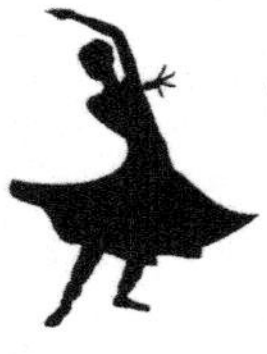

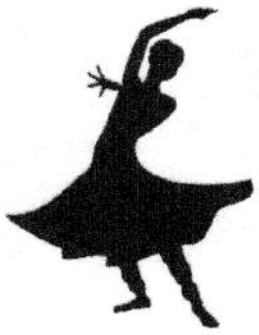

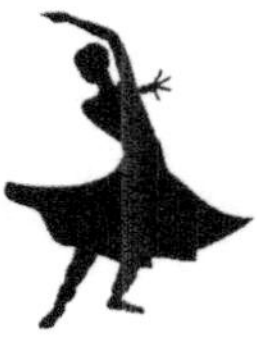

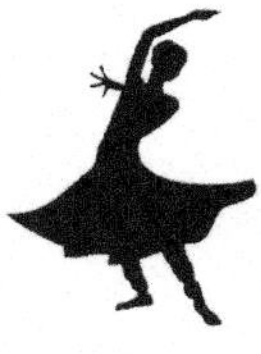

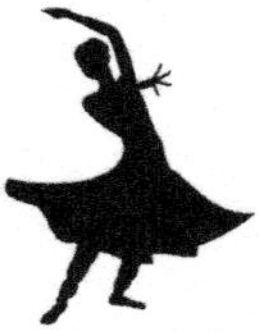

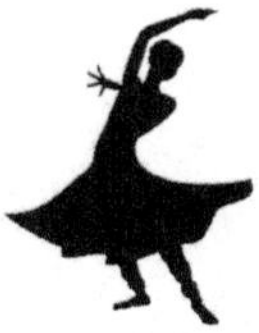

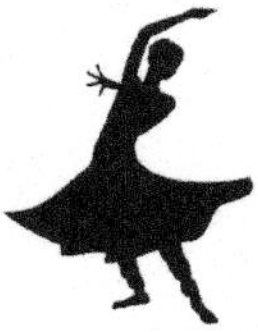

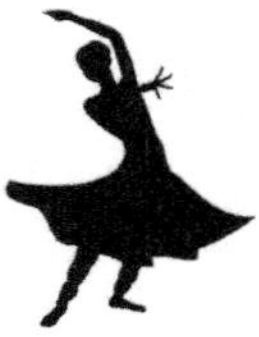

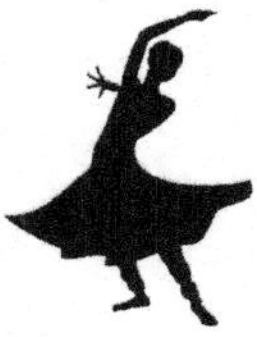

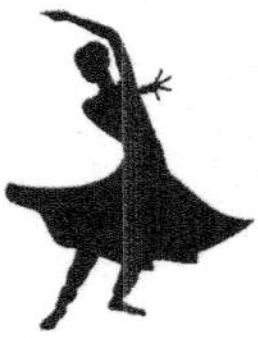

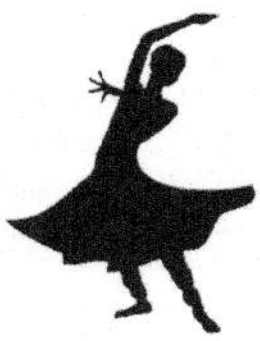

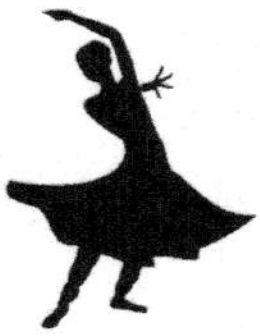

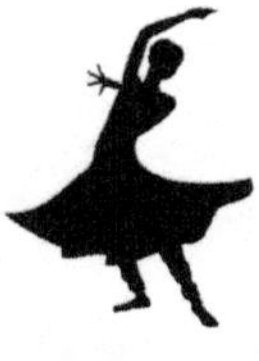

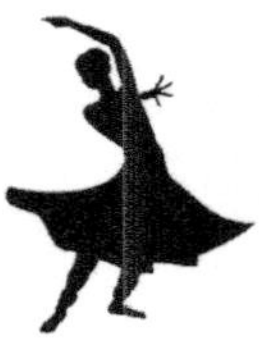

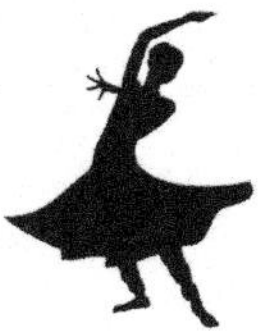

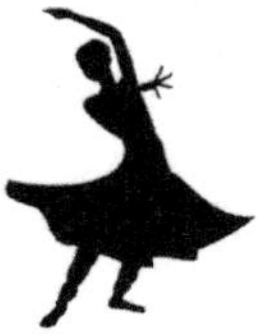

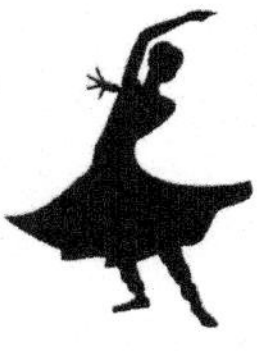

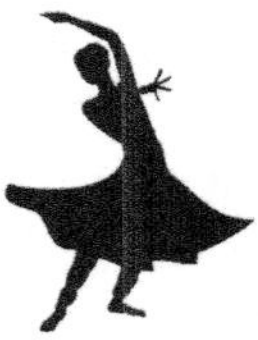

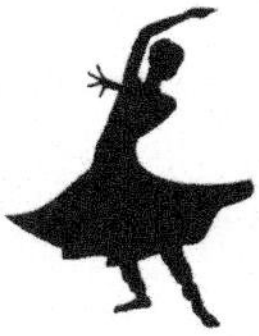

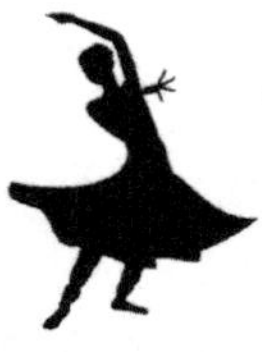

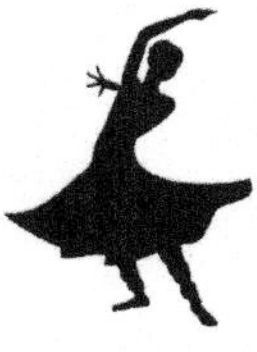

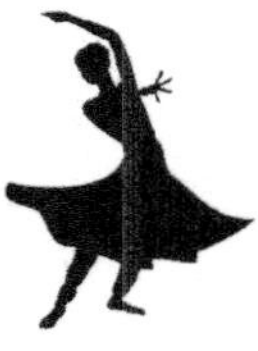

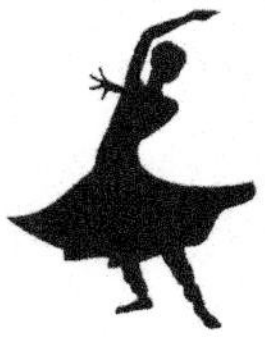

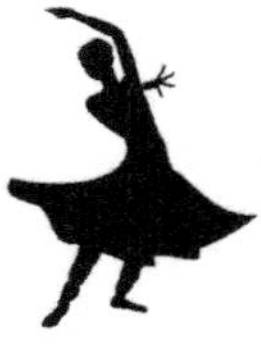

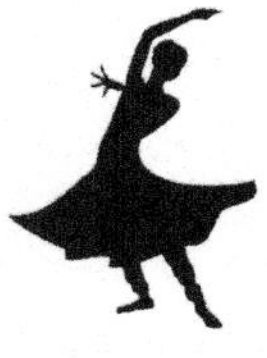

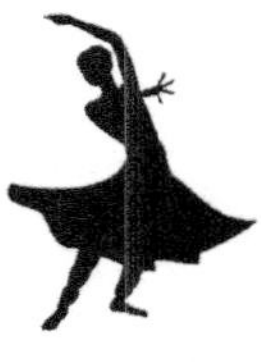

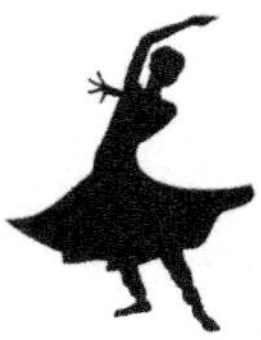

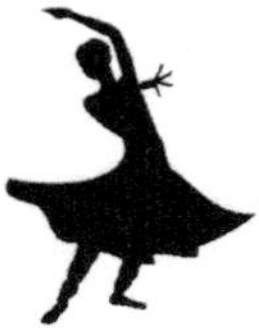

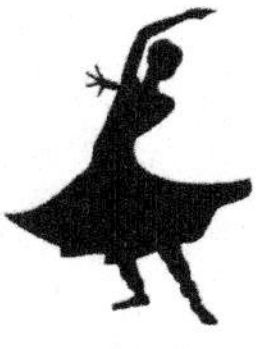

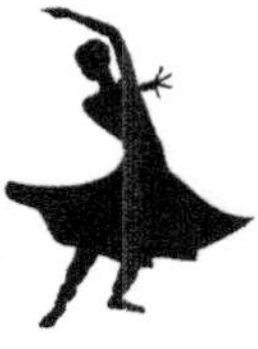

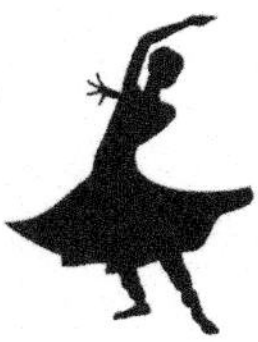

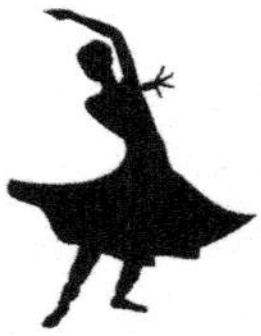

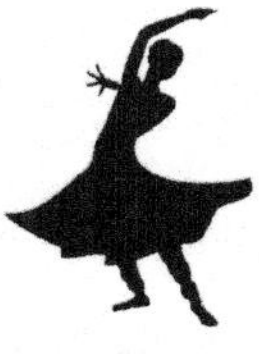

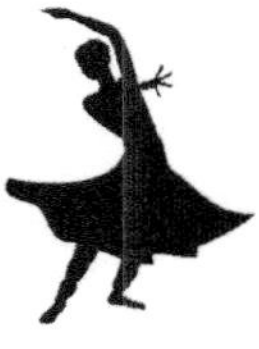

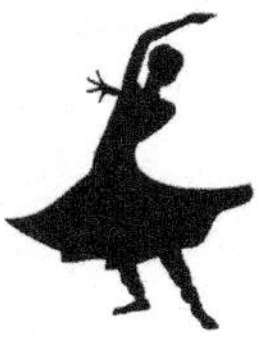

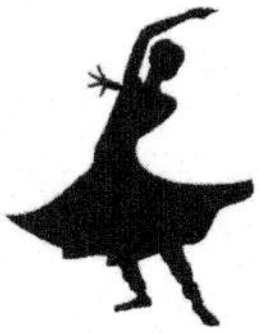

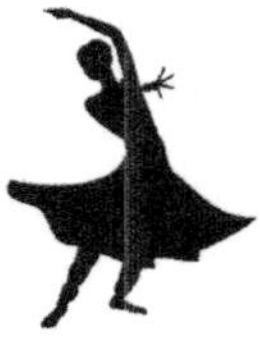

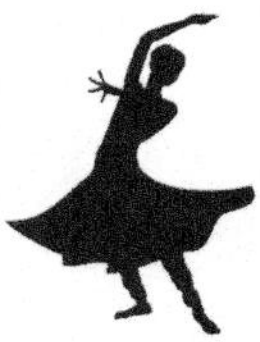

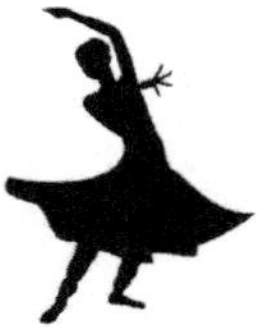

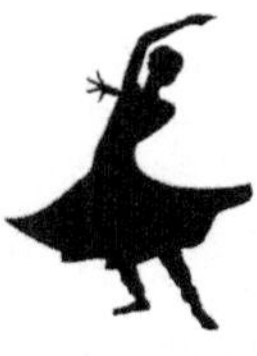

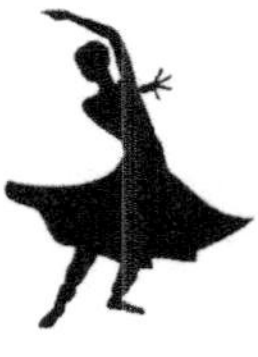

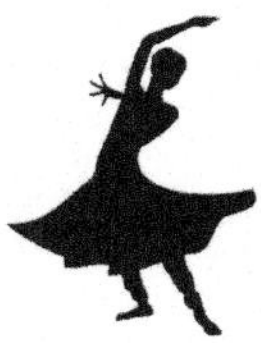

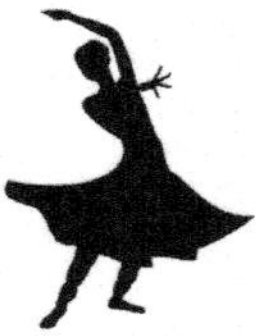

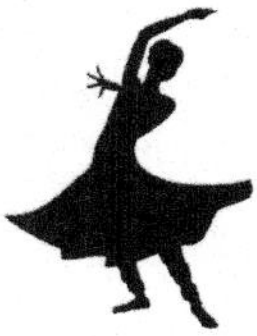

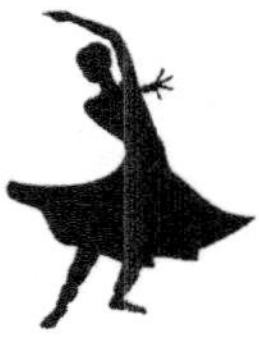

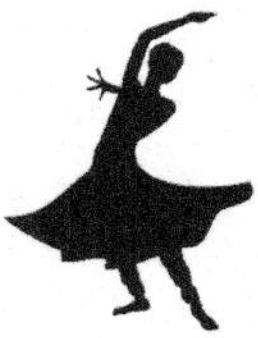

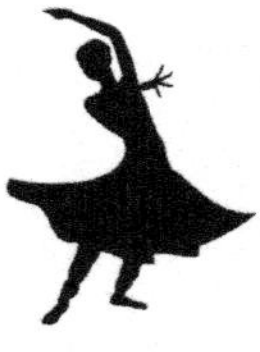

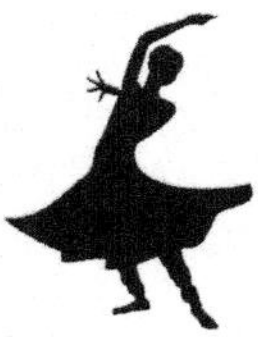

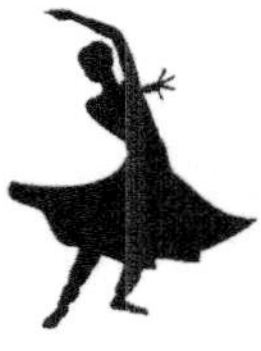

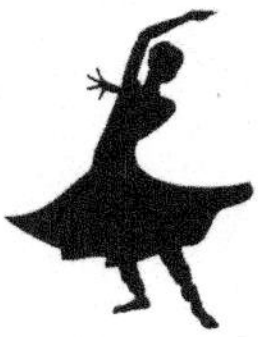

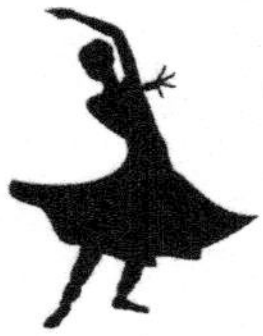

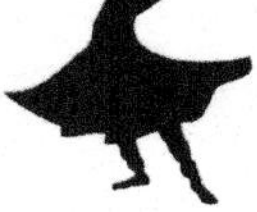

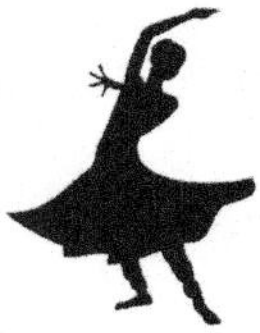

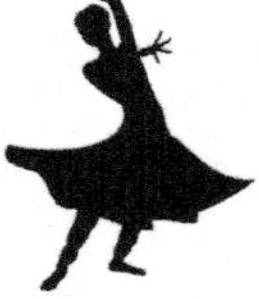

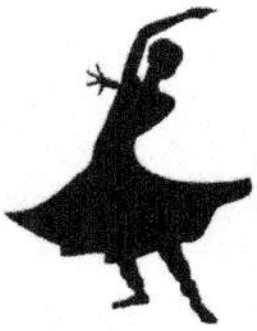

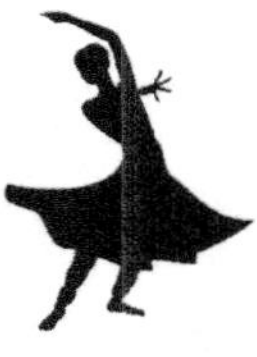

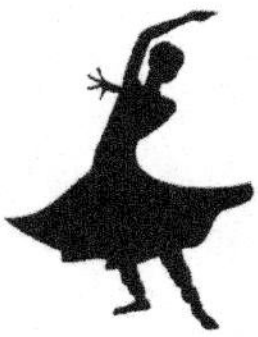

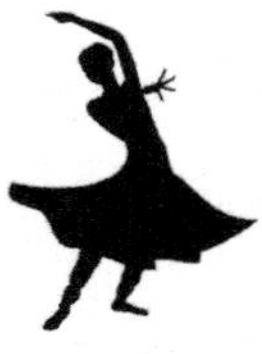

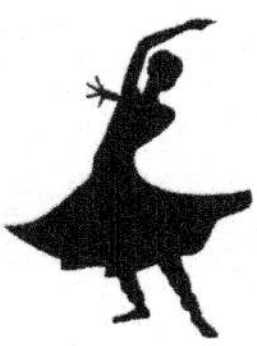

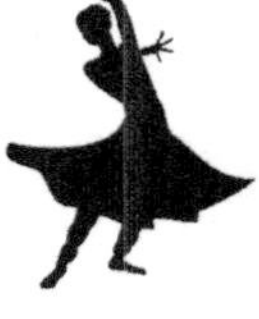

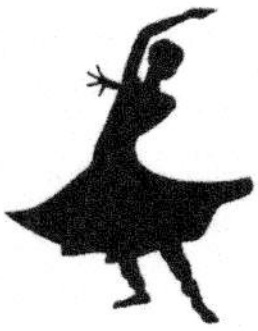

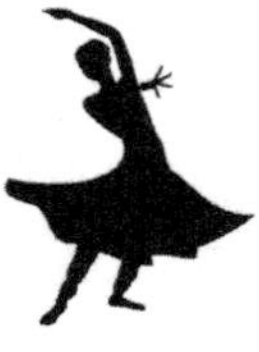

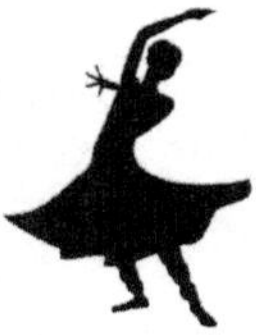

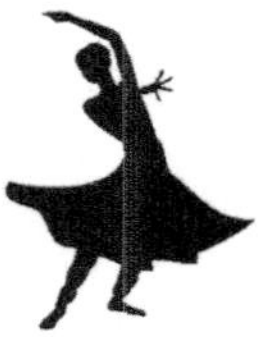

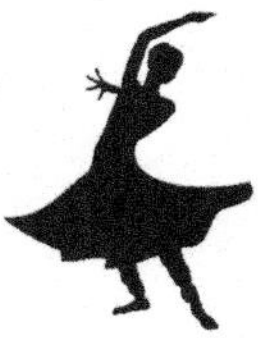

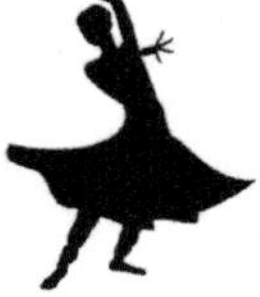

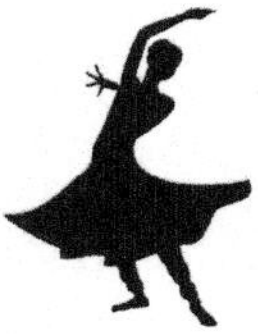

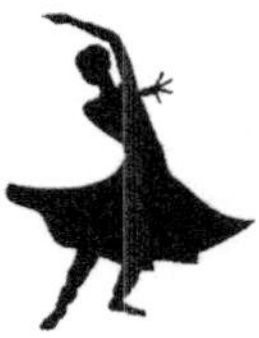

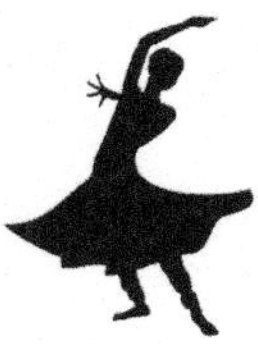

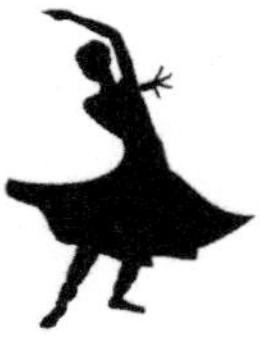

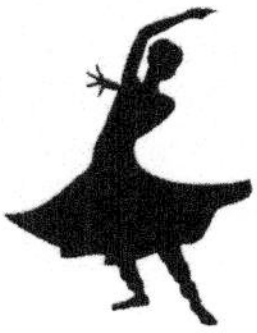

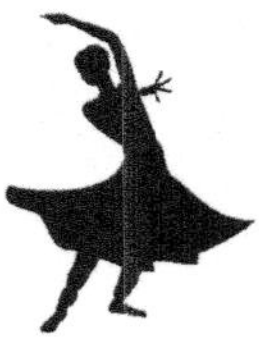

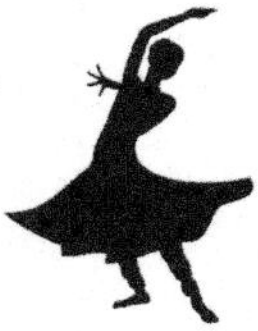

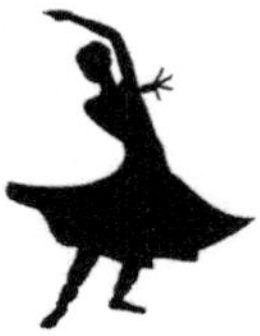

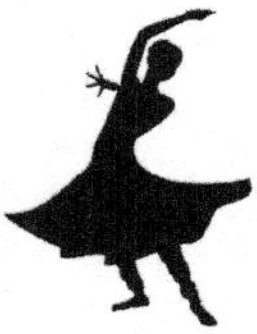

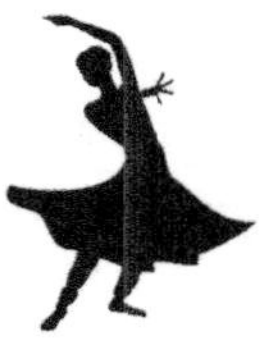

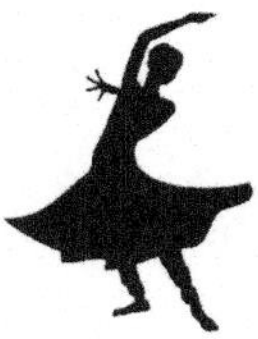

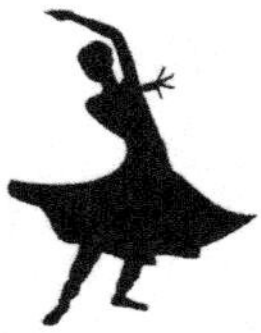

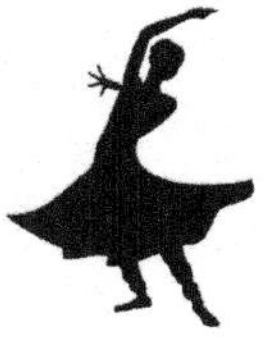

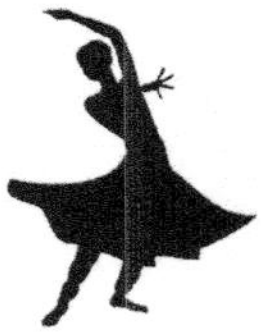

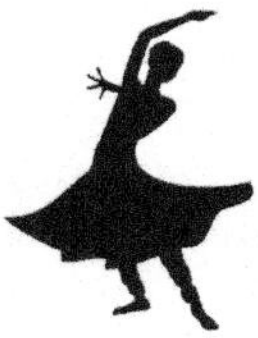

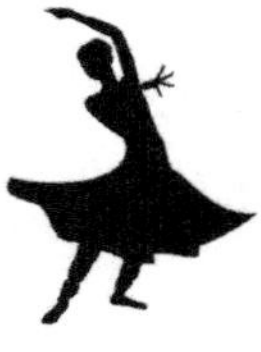

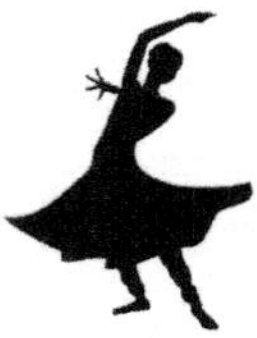

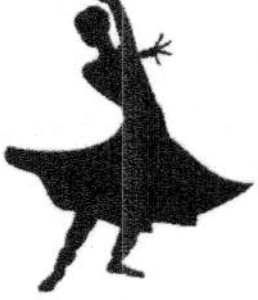

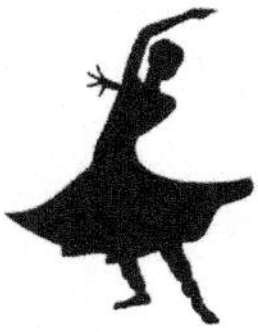

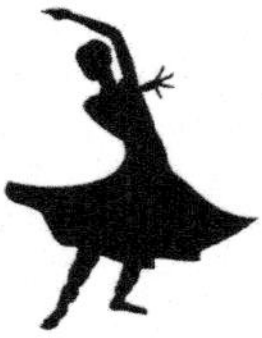

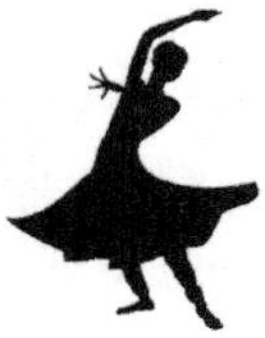

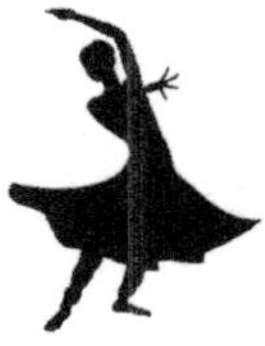

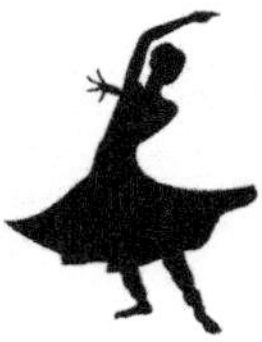

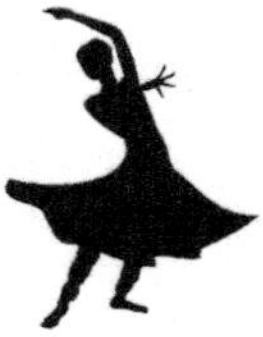

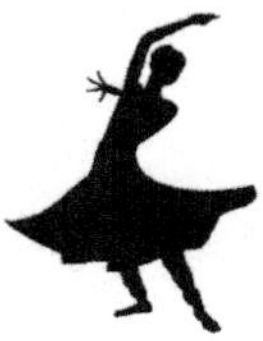

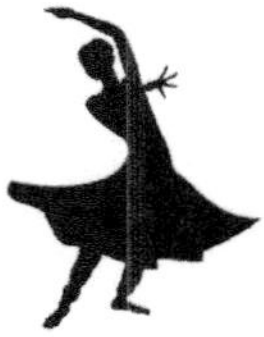

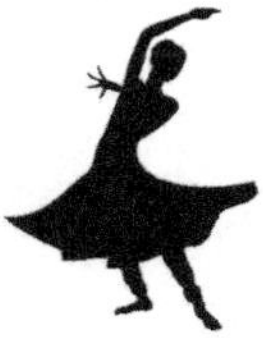

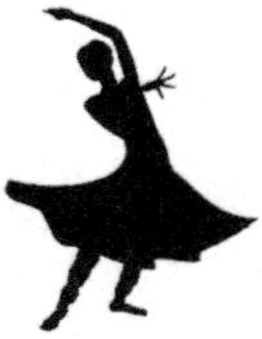

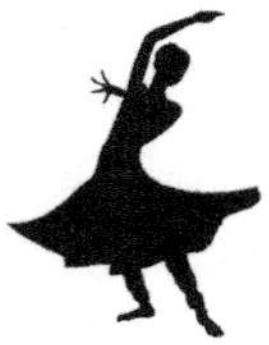

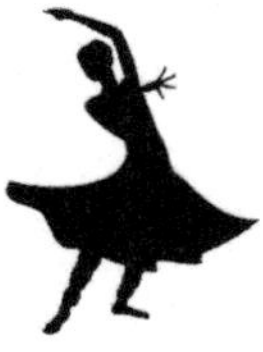

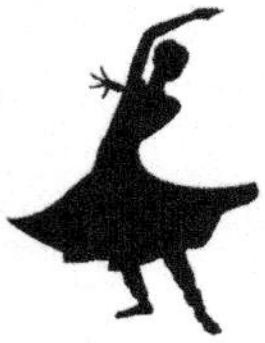

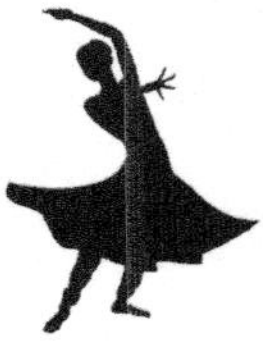

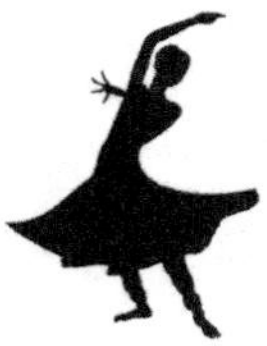

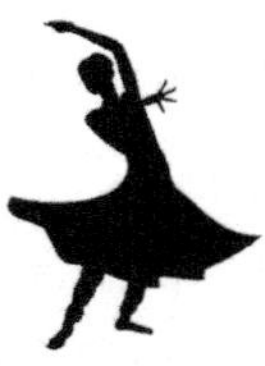

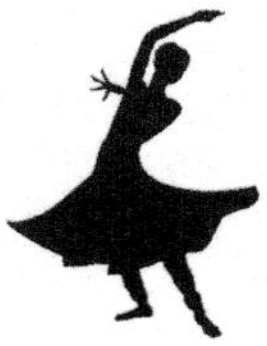

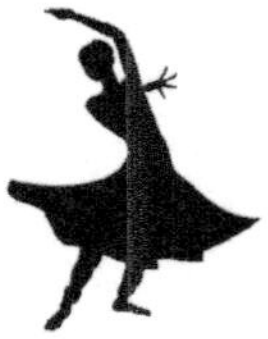

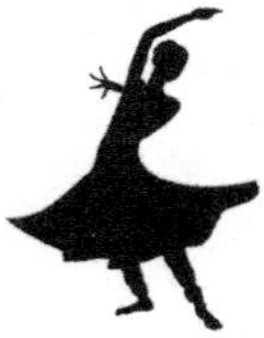

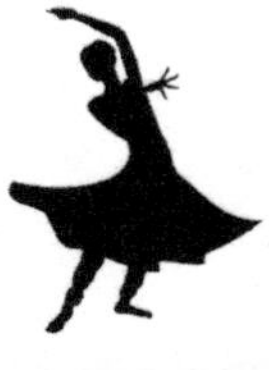

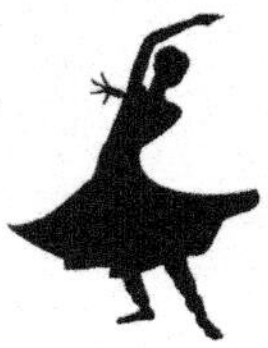

"The way I dance is by writing"

-- Anne Lamott

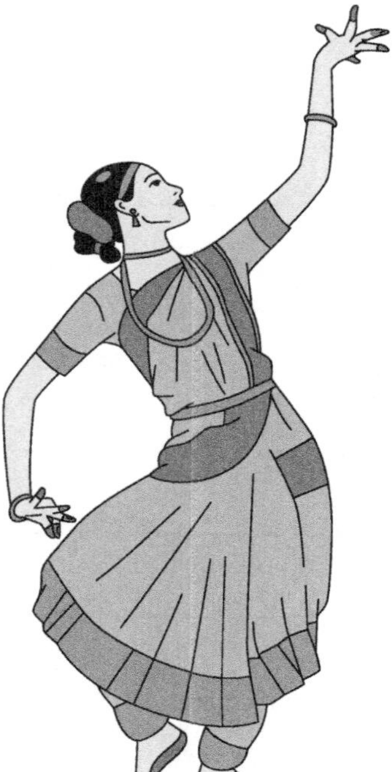

Happy Writing

Printed in Great Britain
by Amazon

26016333R00071